Allen Carr

The illustrated easy way to stop  drinking

Allen Carr

The illustrated easy way to stop

drinking

with
Bev Aisbett

ARCTURUS

ARCTURUS

This edition published in 2015 by Arcturus Publishing Limited
26/27 Bickels Yard, 151–153 Bermondsey Street,
London SE1 3HA, UK

ISBN: 978-1-78404-504-3
AD004271UK

Printed in the UK

Contents

DEDICATIONS

To Crispin Hay, Allen Carr's Easyway to
Stop Drinking Therapist Extraordinaire

To Senna who keeps me merry in the healthiest way

Bev Aisbett is the author and illustrator of 14 self-help books.
Bev has previously illustrated **Allen Carr's Easy Way to Stop
Smoking** and **Allen Carr's Easy Way for Women to
Stop Smoking**.

ALLEN CARR

Allen Carr was a chain-smoker for over 30 years. In 1983, after countless failed attempts to quit, he went from 100 cigarettes a day to zero without suffering withdrawal pangs, without using willpower, and without putting on weight. He realized that he had discovered what the world had been waiting for – the Easy Way to Stop Smoking, and embarked on a mission to help cure the world's smokers.

As a result of the phenomenal success of his method, he gained an international reputation as the world's leading expert on stopping smoking and his network of clinics now spans the globe. His first book, *Allen Carr's Easy Way to Stop Smoking*, has sold over 12 million copies, remains a global best-seller and has been published in over 40 different languages. Hundreds of thousands of smokers have successfully quit at Allen Carr's Easyway Clinics where, with a success rate of over 90%, he guarantees you'll find it easy to stop or your money back.

Allen Carr's Easyway method has been successfully applied to a host of issues including weight control, alcohol and other addictions and fears. A list of Allen Carr clinics appears at the back of this book. Should you require any assistance or if you have any questions, please do not hesitate to contact your nearest clinic.

For more information about Allen Carr's Easyway, please visit

www.allencarr.com

Is
your DRINKING
becoming
a PROBLEM?

If you've picked up this book, then it's likely that drinking – or rather, whether you have **CONTROL** over your drinking – is something of an issue for you.

Well, I'm a LONG-TERM ALCOHOLIC so of COURSE it is!

I consider myself a SOCIAL DRINKER but I do tend to drink quite OFTEN and too MUCH!

If your drinking habits are like those of these people, is the
Easyway method likely to be helpful for you?
ABSOLUTELY!

But there is **_ONE EXCEPTION..._**

It would be preferable if the person who has the **DRINKING PROBLEM** is the one who seeks out this book.

Because it's unlikely to be effective if someone feels **OBLIGATED** to quit. The individual needs to come to this decision because he or she **WANTS** to change and not to please someone else.

So, if you've picked up this book **INDEPENDENTLY** and of your own **FREE WILL**, then you've come to the **RIGHT PLACE**. Even if this book was given to you, you chose to start reading it.

Either way, you'll find that this method is called *Easyway* for good reason!

THE
Easyway
APPROACH

TRUE or FALSE?

- Alcoholism is an **INCURABLE DISEASE**

- Giving up alcohol is **HARD**

- You will suffer **BAD WITHDRAWAL SYMPTOMS**

- Giving up alcohol requires enormous ongoing **WILLPOWER**

- You will feel **DEPRIVED**

- You will have to **SACRIFICE**

- You will have to **RESIST** the **TEMPTATION** to drink for the rest of your life

- An easy, quick and permanent cure is a **FAIRYTALE!**

All the statements above are **FALSE**.

Yes, and this opinion is widely supported by many members of the **MEDICAL PROFESSION**.

While you may have **STRUGGLED** to gain control until now,
here's the

GOOD NEWS!

The _Easyway_ Method is:

- **IMMEDIATE**

- **PERMANENT**

- **FREE OF UNPLEASANT WITHDRAWAL SYMPTOMS**

- **RELY ON WILLPOWER**

- **FEEL DEPRIVED**

- **RESIST TEMPTATION**

- **ENJOY SOCIALIZING MORE**

- **HANDLE STRESS BETTER**

But there's a reason why people from all over the **WORLD** have followed the _Easyway_ method and that's simply because **IT WORKS!**

In the time it takes to **READ** the **BOOK** thoroughly and **FOLLOW THE INSTRUCTIONS**, years of misery, shame and expense will be over **FOR GOOD!**

Imagine you were
IMPRISONED
in a cell with a
COMBINATION LOCK...

...you could spend
YEARS stuck in
there trying to
figure out the
COMBINATION...

…but if someone **GAVE YOU** those numbers you'd be **INSTANTLY FREE!**

Easyway gives you the combination to **UNLOCK** the **PRISON CELL** of alcohol and, in your hands, you now hold the key to **FREEDOM**.

You're ACTUALLY saying that just by READING this BOOK I'll be CURED?

Yes, your problem with drinking is **OVER** once you fully understand the information contained within this book and follow the instructions **TO THE LETTER**.

Not at all!

Just **READ THE BOOK** and **FOLLOW** the simple **INSTRUCTIONS** and the lock is opened.

Simple as that!

Think of each of the instructions as being one of the **NUMBERS** of the **COMBINATION LOCK**. Miss one number and the lock won't open. Key ALL of them in, in the correct sequence, and, **VOILA!**, you're **FREE!**

There are only **SEVEN** instructions and we'll look at them next.

THE
Easyway
INSTRUCTIONS

1. FOLLOW THE INSTRUCTIONS!

There are only **SEVEN** instructions and you will succeed if you follow **ALL** of them.

2. DON'T JUMP THE GUN

Don't **READ AHEAD** or **SKIP SECTIONS** of the book. Read it from **START** to **FINISH**.

3. ONLY READ THE BOOK WHEN YOU'RE SOBER

Remember – you can read it at your own pace!

4. DO NOT QUIT OR CUT DOWN UNTIL YOU'VE FINISHED THE BOOK

Notable exception: if you've already stopped drinking, don't change that.

5. START OFF IN A HAPPY FRAME OF MIND
There's no need to be **MISERABLE!**
Just think how **PROUD** you and your friends and family will
be when you're **FREE**.

You can continue to drink until you've completed the
course, so there's no need to feel that you're not ready yet.
AND: be assured – the Easyway method **WORKS!**

6. QUESTION YOUR ASSUMPTIONS
ABOUT ALCOHOL
There are many **MISCONCEPTIONS** about drinking and
addiction to alcohol that you may have held as 'gospel'.

If you had evidence to the contrary, might you change your
mind? We think so.

And finally, on this point, all we ask is that you:

7. KEEP AN OPEN MIND AND THINK POSITIVELY
This can be the most difficult of the instructions to keep, but
the best way to see if something **WORKS** is to **TEST** it out
for yourself.

If you don't even **TRY**, you'll never know. What do you have
to **LOSE** except a huge **PROBLEM**? This method is called
EASYWAY for a reason!

Not at **ALL** – but you could say it's a type of **COUNTER-BRAINWASHING!**

It involves **REVERSING** beliefs that you may have held for some time and you currently view as **FACTS!**

The false **ASSUMPTIONS** and **ASSERTIONS** that you and even some so-called **EXPERTS** hold about **ALCOHOL**, **ADDICTION** and your **RELATIONSHIP** to these.

First up, let's take a close look at your
'**BEST BUDDY**' – alcohol.

Choose Your POISON

Let's start by looking at some **PROPERTIES** of **ALCOHOL**.

It's an **ANAESTHETIC** and can be burnt as **FUEL**.

It's a **DEPRESSANT**, a **DIURETIC**

 and a **DISINFECTANT**.

ALCOHOL IS A DRUG.

The side-effects of this drug are:

LOSS OF CONTROL
– ranging from phoney affection to risk-taking or violent behaviour.

INEBRIATION
(dictionary definition: deprived of ordinary use of senses and reason).

DAMAGE to the
VITAL ORGANS
(especially the brain
and liver).

Let's get something **STRAIGHT**:
ALCOHOL IS A DEADLY POISON –
nothing **MORE**, nothing **LESS**!

Though we
attempt to
GLAMORIZE it...

...and 90% of the world's population uses it...

...and its use (and abuse) has been **NORMALIZED** for **CENTURIES**...

...there's no getting around the fact that it can make you **BROKE, SAD, LONELY, SICK** AND **_DEAD!_**

Would you buy this 'fabulous product'*?

INTRODUCING

our wonderful new product…
EXHILARATION!

POWERFUL POISON! **HIGHLY ADDICTIVE!** **RUINS YOUR IMMUNE SYSTEM!**

ERODES CONFIDENCE! **WRECKS YOUR NERVOUS SYSTEM!** **TASTES AWFUL!**

AND! IT WILL ONLY COST YOU
BETWEEN **£100,000 & £142,000**
IN YOUR LIFETIME!

PLUS!!

IT WILL DO **ABSOLUTELY NOTHING** FOR YOU!

Strangely, lots of people do.

(*Of course, this '**_Fabulous Product_**' is ALCOHOL!)

You only say that because the drug that is alcohol is **LEGAL**!

And because so many people **DRINK**!

Besides, heroin pushers aren't allowed to **ADVERTISE**!

We lightly toss around the terms we use to describe drunkenness as if they didn't accurately reflect the true nature of the **DAMAGE** alcohol inflicts:

LEGLESS, PARALYTIC, BLIND, BOMBED, HAMMERED, SLAUGHTERED, SMASHED, TRASHED, ANNIHILATED, WRECKED, WASTED

The only reason we fail to see **ALCOHOL** as being as **DANGEROUS** as heroin or other drugs of addiction is that we see heroin as **EVIL** and **ALCOHOL** use as **NORMAL**.

SPOT THE DIFFERENCE:
which **DRUG** does more **DAMAGE?**

The question is: why do you need an **ARTIFICIAL** lift?

A DRUG is not **NATURAL** for your body.

When 'normal' drinkers are given something to celebrate, say a **PARTY**, a **PAY RISE** or a **HOLIDAY**, they immediately start drinking!

Then **WHY** are you reading this book? If you can **LEAVE** it, why **TAKE** it?

You obviously still think alcohol **DOES SOMETHING** for you, which is an **ILLUSION**.

Or is it because they've been **TRICKED** into thinking it's enjoyable? (We'll look at that more closely later.)

That's part of the **BRAINWASHING** that **ALCOHOL** creates (we'll look at that soon, too).

Have you noticed that before alcohol **STARTS TO DESTROY YOUR LIFE**, there's no desire to **QUIT**?

Only when it's started to cause real **DAMAGE** do people wish they had more **CONTROL** over their drinking.

Stupidity doesn't come into it.

That's why so many people who have a **DRINKING PROBLEM** (are or were) **GO-GETTERS** and **BUSINESS LEADERS**.

Surely someone becomes a **HEAVY DRINKER** by **CHOICE!**

Then why is it so hard, even for an occasional drinker, to **CUT** down or **QUIT?**

But isn't an awareness of the **DANGERS** enough to rein it in?

ALCOHOL MURDER SPREE

STAR DIES OF BOOZE BINGE

DRINK CAR SMASH

LIVER DAMAGE KILLS

NO! That just **SCARES** people into drinking **MORE!**

HOW SO?

The more you focus on the **DAMAGE**, the more people **FREAK OUT!**

The more **TRAPPED** you feel –
the more you drink, and the worse it gets.

And the more you focus on the **DANGERS**, the more your
mind argues that there are **REASONS** why you **DRINK**.

Such as:

You conclude that
alcohol must do
SOMETHING for you
or you wouldn't drink.

39

You already **KNOW** what damage alcohol can do to:

- **HEALTH**

- **FAMILY**

- **FRIENDSHIPS**

- **FINANCES**

- **SELF-RESPECT**

And even if you don't, would it be **HELPFUL** to know more **HORROR FACTS**?

NO!

It would just **SCARE** you into drinking **MORE**.

Think back to the **PRISON CELL** (the one you don't yet have the combination to unlock).

Would focusing on how **BAD** it is to be in there help you to escape?

Perhaps the more accurate word is '**DESPERATE**'!

But the question:

...doesn't open the lock either.

The question:

...**DOES!**

41

So would you say that the distinction between an **'ALCOHOLIC'** and a **'SOCIAL DRINKER'** is that an alcoholic is a drinker who has **LOST CONTROL?**

So at what point does the drinker **LOSE CONTROL?**

Here's the thing – they (and you) were **_NEVER_** in **CONTROL!**

You've been **BRAINWASHED** from the start! Let's see how.

The Brainwashing

Right from our earliest years, we have been bombarded with messages that alcohol is a **NORMAL PART OF LIFE**...

...and that it's an **ESSENTIAL** component of **SOCIAL INTERACTION**.

We grew up with **ALCOHOL** as a feature in the **FILMS** we watched…

…the **BOOKS** we read…

…and in the endless **ADVERTISING** that bombarded us daily.

No wonder it's taken such a hold!

The image of **ALCOHOL** to which we have been subjected perpetuates the **MYTHS** that alcohol:

- Makes us **HAPPY**

- Steadies the **NERVES**

- Eases physical and emotional **PAIN**

- Helps us **RELAX**

- Makes us **SEXIER**

- Is essential for **SOCIALIZING**

Our drinking is acceptable as long as we remain **ENTERTAINING** or **HAPPY** drunks.

But should we become **PATHETIC**, **MISERABLE** or **AGGRESSIVE** drunks, our family and friends start to **MAKE EXCUSES** for us:

And we make **EXCUSES** for our own loss of control.

47

We still fail to see an alcoholic who has reached rock bottom as someone with a terrible **DISEASE** who has no **CHOICE**.

No one deliberately **CHOOSES** to:

RUIN THEIR LIFE

DESTROY THEIR RELATIONSHIPS or **BLOW THEIR FINANCES**

CRUSH THEIR SELF-ESTEEM or **MAKE THEMSELVES ILL...**

...any more than they **CHOOSE** to drink.

Becoming a drinker was **INEVITABLE** in our culture. We were **BRAINWASHED** into doing it and made to feel like an **OUTSIDER** if we didn't.

Imagine you were an alien who had never even **HEARD** of alcohol, let alone **CONSUMED** it, and one day you stumbled into 'civilization'.

48

Then someone
poured alcohol
down your throat…

…and you found
you couldn't
MOVE, THINK, SEE
or **HEAR** properly.

How would that feel?

It would be

TERRIFYING!

So what is the difference between the first experience of
drinking for this alien and our own?

He wasn't **BRAINWASHED** into drinking!

No one had told him that alcohol was a
'**NORMAL**' part of life...

...or that he
would be a
SOCIAL MISFIT if
he didn't drink...

...or that he would
be '**MISSING
SOMETHING**'
without alcohol...

...so he didn't even **THINK** about drinking as an option,
whereas we are bombarded with a lifelong **SALES PITCH**
about its merits from many different quarters.

The alcohol trap laid out for us is **SEDUCTIVE**. Some people
escape while others are rendered completely **HELPLESS** –
just like a fly in a **PITCHER PLANT**.

The TRAP

This trap of addiction is both **POWERFUL** and **SUBTLE**.

Let's take a look at how this works by using the example of the **FLY** and the **PITCHER PLANT**.

Here's the fly happily buzzing along.

It doesn't **NEED** anything to feel complete – nature has provided abundantly to sustain the fly's existence.

But on this particular day, the fly happens to spot an **UNUSUAL, EXOTIC** and **ENTICING BLOOM** and it gets curious.

The fly goes **EXPLORING**…

…only to find that this trip is **ONE WAY!**

However, the fly isn't particularly **BOTHERED** by the fact – so far he's having a **GRAND OLD TIME!**

But after some time the fly finds himself getting a bit **FED UP** with this.

What started off as **ENJOYABLE** is now making him feel **SICK**...

...and it is then it dawns on him that something **BAD** is starting to happen here...

...he realizes that the delicious nectar he was eating has started to **EAT HIM!**

ALL DRINKERS are like that fly at various stages of descent inside the plant:

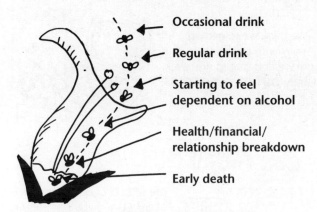

- Occasional drink
- Regular drink
- Starting to feel dependent on alcohol
- Health/financial/ relationship breakdown
- Early death

Any fly entering this trap is in danger of falling **ALL THE WAY**.

Even the teenager taking a first sip is at risk of immediately becoming **TRAPPED**.

Hmm- your HOBBY will become your CAREER!

Teenagers, in particular, want to **BELONG** and drinking is a major part of youth culture.

The question is: will the early drinking continue into **ADULTHOOD**?

The insidious part of this process is that our slide happens so **SLOWLY** we don't **NOTICE** it at first.

We think we're getting away with our drinking until we find that things are already **OUT OF CONTROL.**

The **SPEED** of descent is often **SLOWED** only by **EXTERNAL CONSTRAINTS** such as:

FAMILY COMMITMENTS,

UPHOLDING A REPUTATION,

CLUB PRESIDENT

REPORT DEADLINE

MAINTAINING A CAREER,

...but while these things may slow the **RATE OF DESCENT**, nonetheless, you're still in the trap.

Be honest – if you could **DRINK MORE** and still hold on to your job, your family and your reputation, **YOU WOULD**, wouldn't you?

The most sinister aspect of this trap is that it creates several **ILLUSIONS**:

THAT DRINKING IS ENJOYABLE

THAT PEOPLE CHOOSE TO DRINK

THAT ALCOHOL TASTES GOOD

THAT ALCOHOL EASES STRESS

THAT ALCOHOL GIVES YOU COURAGE

THAT ALCOHOL IS AN ADJUNCT TO SOCIALIZING

AND **THAT QUITTING IS DIFFICULT!**

When did the fly realize he was trapped?

It was when he had had enough nectar to feel **SICK**...

...and realized it was creating **PROBLEMS**.

It just didn't feel **GOOD** any more...

...and he wanted to **FLY AWAY**...

...but he was well and truly **STUCK!**

This is the stage when you start getting
HINTS from family and friends...

...or someone
WINCES at your
BOOZY BREATH...

...or you've
SMASHED UP
the **CAR**...

...blown your
WAGES...

...or **DISGRACED** yourself – _AGAIN_!

You're still in **DENIAL** but you
KNOW there's a **PROBLEM**.

So you set out to **PROVE** that you have **CONTROL**
by **CUTTING DOWN**.

Something **CRITICAL** has now happened.

Up till now you drank with **IMPUNITY** and now you've decided you need to **CUT BACK**...

...but still you associate '**SPECIAL OCCASIONS**' or certain activities with **DRINKING**...

...and without **ALCOHOL** you feel **DEPRIVED**.

So on the occasions when you allow yourself a drink...

...it quickly
becomes
SEVERAL or
MANY.

The part of your brain that made you want to drink
with **ABANDON** doesn't change because you realize
you have a **PROBLEM!**

In fact, the more you feel **DEPRIVED** of something,
the more you tend to **DESIRE** it.

Ask any dieter!

Once you realize you have a **PROBLEM**...

...you gain a **SECOND** problem!

You're now caught between drinking **TOO MUCH**...

...and constantly feeling deprived...

...which creates a mighty internal **STRUGGLE!**

Of course, the more you **STRUGGLE**, the more **TRAPPED** you become...

...and the more **PRECIOUS** that drink seems.

It now seems there's only **ONE** way to regain **CONTROL**...

WILLPOWER

...if only it actually **WORKED**!

Why WILLPOWER is really WON'T POWER

If you can just summon enough **WILLPOWER** you can **QUIT**, right?

How **HARD** can it be?

As it turns out, not only is using the **WILLPOWER** method the **HARD** way to quit, it's seldom **SUCCESSFUL** because it ingrains the idea that you can **NEVER BE CURED**!

Actually, **NO**.

You may have **STOPPED DRINKING**…

…but you're **FAR** from **CURED**.

You still **WANT** to drink, don't you?

Then you're just a **DRINKER** who's **NOT ALLOWED TO DRINK!**

71

The **BIG** question is:
HOW LONG CAN YOU HOLD OUT?

Having to exercise **WILLPOWER** and fight **CRAVINGS** for a **LIFETIME** is a **HEFTY DEMAND!**

Are you really **UP FOR THAT?**

But you'll only feel that way if you believe you're **LOSING** something. Applying **WILLPOWER** means you're constantly fighting to contain the craving for what you've 'lost'.

Expressions such as *'give up'*, *'deny yourself'*, *'forgo'* or *'withhold'* all create the sense you're making a **SACRIFICE**.

Merely **CONTEMPLATING** giving up is enough to fill you with **DOOM** and **GLOOM!**

The longer you **HOLD OUT**, the more you forget the **MISERY** that prompted you to quit in the first place.

So, once again there's that **TEMPTATION** to have…

And, **HEY PRESTO!**, you're **TRAPPED** again! And all this because you think alcohol **DOES SOMETHING** for you.

Let's banish that illusion **ONCE** and **FOR ALL!**

EXCUSES, EXCUSES

The **EXCUSES** for drinking fall into three
MAIN CATEGORIES:

• **PHYSICAL**

• **PSYCHOLOGICAL**

• **SOCIAL**

Let's explore these one by one:

<u>**PHYSICAL**</u>

You didn't when you
STARTED, did you?

Most of us were weaned on to alcohol by
adding a sweetener.

Think back to
your first taste of
alcohol.

This is your body saying: **WARNING! POISON! STOP!**

Remember the first time alcohol made you **SICK?**

If a **FOOD** did that to you, wouldn't you **AVOID** it?

But no, we **DRINK** again…

…and **AGAIN** despite all the **REASONS** not to.

77

Our **NATURAL INSTINCT** is to be
REPELLED by alcohol. Give a child a taste
of **NEAT SPIRIT** and they'll spit it out!

It's not the **ALCOHOL**
itself that gives the
TASTE you enjoy
– it's the other
INGREDIENTS that
are **ADDED** to make it
PALATABLE.

If alcohol tasted good by itself,
why would there be any need to
DISGUISE the taste?

We have to **WORK HARD** to acquire the taste for alcohol.

Are there no **NON-ALCOHOLIC** drinks that you also enjoy?

So obviously you're not drinking **MORE** just because you like the **TASTE** of the drink.

Why then do you **KEEP ON DRINKING ALCOHOL?**

79

Is it?

ALCOHOL is a
DIURETIC...

...which is a drug
that reduces the
amount of **WATER**
in the body.

In other words – **IT DRIES YOU OUT!**

That's why you wake
up after a binge utterly
PARCHED.

Instead of **QUENCHING** your thirst, alcohol **CREATES** it.

Would you need *16 PINTS* of **WATER** to
satisfy your **THIRST**?

Yet on a **BINGE** some people drink that amount of **ALCOHOL**.

QUENCHING THIRST has nothing to do with it.

If it's **ANTIOXIDANTS** you're after, why choose **ALCOHOL** as the source? There are plenty of **FOODS** that contain them that won't **POISON** you at the same time.

Besides, if alcohol is **HEALTHY**, why do people **STAGGER**, **PASS OUT**, **VOMIT** and wake up feeling like **DEATH**?

Half a pint of pure alcohol will **KILL** you!

Think of your **FAVOURITE FOOD**.

Let's say, for some crazy reason, you ate enough of this food in one go to make yourself **SICK**.

Would you be rushing off to get **MORE** that **VERY DAY**?

But that's what you'd do if you had a **DRINKING PROBLEM**, isn't it?

PSYCHOLOGICAL

This is a common belief but true mental relaxation is an **ALERT** state.

Relaxation isn't achieved by trying to **OBLITERATE** cares and worries; it's knowing you can effectively handle **WHATEVER** life throws at you.

You can't do that when you're **HALF-SHOT**.

Alcohol may literally **ANAESTHETIZE** you (by rendering you unconscious), but when you come to, you're still aware of problems and now you've added even **MORE** with your drinking.

ALCOHOL puts a **BLANKET** over stress but doesn't address the **CAUSE**.

Stress will remain until the **CAUSE** of the stress is remedied.

And if you're **DRINKING** to control the stress then the stress is **ALREADY** out of control.

Then what do you have? **MORE STRESS**!

And you end up in a **VICIOUS** cycle.

But surely a few drinks to UNWIND after a STRESSFUL WORK DAY doesn't do any HARM!

The question is why **AREN'T** you already **RELAXED**?
What's **REALLY** causing the **UNREST**?

DEADLINES
MONEY WORRIES
JOB INSECURITY
MORTGAGE

Alcohol **DEADENS** your **SENSES**. It doesn't remove **PROBLEMS**; it just makes you momentarily **OBLIVIOUS** to them.

If you were **CONTENT** in yourself, you wouldn't need a **DRINK** to relax you.

If alcohol **REALLY** made you happy, you wouldn't need to keep **TOPPING UP**.

Alcohol is a **TEMPORARY FIX** – in fact, it isn't even that: it just makes things **WORSE**!

But I find I CAN cope better with STRESS after a few DRINKS!

CAN you?

Say you've had a **STRESSFUL DAY** and you stop off for a few drinks.

Then your wife calls: your child is ill and needs to go to hospital **IMMEDIATELY**.

Do you feel any **LESS** stressed about the situation?

Wouldn't you feel even **MORE** stressed knowing that your ability to **FUNCTION** is impaired?

Like many people, you may have a fear of **FLYING**.

No matter how many pre-flight drinks you have, **GUESS WHAT**?

The minute you step on board the plane you're **STONE-COLD SOBER!**

> But surely a little *DUTCH COURAGE* takes the *EDGE* off things?

And what do you need **COURAGE** for?

To overcome

FEAR.

We'll do **ANYTHING** to avoid feeling **FEAR** but **FEAR** is nature's way of keeping us **SAFE** from **HARM**.

Fear ensures we take **PRECAUTIONS**.

> Better *TAKE CARE* with this *LADDER!*

> This is *FLAMMABLE* - better store it *SAFELY!*

> I'll wear my *LIFEJACKET!*

89

Alcohol **DULLS** your **SENSES** so it isn't a matter of giving you **COURAGE**, but rather taking away **FEAR**.

Removing fear increases your susceptibility to **DANGER**.

It's like believing you can put out the fire by turning off the **ALARM**.

When you use alcohol to remove fear, you turn off the **ALARM**.

The fire is still **RAGING**, but now you can **IGNORE IT**.

There's no difference between making yourself **'BLIND DRUNK'** and sticking your head in the sand.

Alcohol doesn't make you **FEARLESS**.
It makes you **RECKLESS**.

When you drink to cope with life, you cannot face life on its **OWN TERMS**.

Therefore **ALCOHOL** actually **DESTROYS** courage.

SOCIAL

Have you ever considered that **SHYNESS** can be a very **ATTRACTIVE** quality?

There's really nothing more **TEDIOUS** than a **BLOW-HARD** – especially one with a few **DRINKS** on board!

Often **SHYNESS** can be overcome by shifting the attention from **YOURSELF** to **OTHERS**.

All it usually takes is a couple of questions about people's **JOBS**, **HOBBIES** or **KIDS**, and they're **OFF**!

And meanwhile, you've **FORGOTTEN** you're **SHY**!

INHIBITION serves a purpose: it tells us when **ENOUGH** is **ENOUGH**.

When you lose **INHIBITION** you don't know when to…

…curtail **AGGRESSION**…

…end an **ARGUMENT**…

...recognize that you're **BORING** someone **SENSELESS**...

...exercise **RESTRAINT**...

...refrain from **DANGEROUS ACTIVITIES**...

...or save yourself from appearing **FOOLISH**.

Without **INHIBITION** you fail to...

...recognize **DANGER**...

...or be **DISCERNING**.

Does your drinking actually help you **BLEND IN** or does it cause you to **STICK OUT** like a **SORE THUMB**?

Unless, of course, everyone else is also
BLOTTO, in which case, none of you is
going to **REMEMBER** much about this
'GREAT TIME' you've had.

And if you **DON'T** remember what you enjoyed, then what
was the **POINT** of **DOING** it?

And, if you can only find your **BLOTTO** friends fun when you're **BLOTTO** too, it may be an idea to think again about who you're hanging out with.

Notice that you're not saying, 'because I **ENJOY** it'.

If you felt **GOOD** about your drinking why would you need to **JUSTIFY** it?

Having to **VALIDATE** your drinking also suggests you know you have a **PROBLEM**.

Do you really want to be one of the **HERD**, mindlessly ruining your health just to **FIT IN**?

Admittedly, drinkers can be **PUSHY**! Alcohol is the only drink people **INSIST** that you share with them.

Imagine if the following was about **PINEAPPLE JUICE**:

Why this **INSISTENCE** that you join in?

Because even the **ILLUSION** of pleasure disappears when the drinker has to drink **ALONE**.

Here's what alcohol does for you:

NOTHING

The REAL reason you drink

Well, I can see now that there is no *BENEFIT* from drinking but why do I still feel like I *NEED* to drink?

Quite simply because you feel **DEPENDENT** on the **DRUG** that is **ALCOHOL**.

You need to keep the **DRUG** topped up in your system, nothing more.

There are no **BENEFITS** to be derived from alcohol. Alcohol does not **HELP** you in any way. It just makes you want **MORE ALCOHOL**.

It just **FEEDS** your **ADDICTION** and keeps it **ALIVE**.

THE SOLE 'PLEASURE' OF DRINKING IS RELIEVING THE CRAVING FOR ALCOHOL TO GET RID OF THE WITHDRAWAL.

So why would I become ADDICTED in the first place? It doesn't happen to EVERYONE who tries DRINKING!

Because you were brainwashed into believing you needed it and that you had some kind of **VOID** or **HOLE** in yourself that you thought **ALCOHOL** would fill.

Alcohol **CREATED** the void and it just makes it **BIGGER**.

It's true - I feel INADEQUATE a lot of the time. But even though I sensed that alcohol wasn't the ANSWER, I kept DRINKING. Why?

You were actually trying to get back to the level of **WELLBEING** you knew **BEFORE** you started drinking.

By DRINKING?! How does THAT work?

Let's take a look…

103

...here's the level of your **WELLBEING** on a good day before you ever started **DRINKING**...

...then, one **FATEFUL DAY**, came the arrival of the **TERRIBLE TWINS!**

THE *LITTLE* MONSTER...

...is a mild, empty, insecure feeling; barely noticeable. It's the feeling of alcohol withdrawal. It appears after your first drink and it makes you want another.

THE *BIG* MONSTER...

...is the **BRAINWASHING**. You've been convinced that you're not **COMPLETE** without alcohol or you think that life can't be **FUN**, you can't **RELAX**, or cope with **STRESS** without it.

THE LITTLE MONSTER gets hungry after each drink as alcohol withdraws from your body.

He demands to be **FED**...

...and when he's **HUNGRY**, you immediately feel **STRESSED**.

His highly protective brother, **THE BIG MONSTER**, convinces you that **ALL WILL BE WELL** if you just keep **FEEDING** that hunger...

...and, indeed, this **SEEMS** to be true, because **THE LITTLE MONSTER** immediately settles down when you have a drink.

And you feel better than you did a moment before.

But it's not long before he's **HUNGRY** again and, once more, you experience that **INSECURE, HOLLOW** feeling...

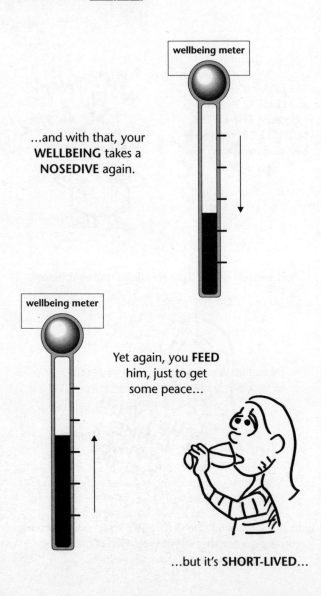

...and with that, your **WELLBEING** takes a **NOSEDIVE** again.

Yet again, you **FEED** him, just to get some peace...

...but it's **SHORT-LIVED**...

...and you can hardly believe it when he's
DEMANDING to be **FED** again!

**THERE IS _NO END_ TO THIS HUNGER. YOU CAN
NEVER, EVER FEED HIM ENOUGH TO STOP THE
CRAVING.**

You could drink a **MILLION, TRILLION DRINKS** and still
crave '**JUST ONE MORE**'!

And, while you continue to drink alcohol, you will
NEVER, EVER reach the level of **WELLBEING** you
experienced before you started.

**EACH DRINK PERPETUATES THE FEELING –
IT DOESN'T RELIEVE IT!!**

But the <u>**REAL**</u> problem is **THE BIG MONSTER**
(the brainwashing).

The **LITTLE MONSTER** (the addiction) is actually a very
mild feeling.

It's this fellow,

BIG MONSTER,

that causes the real discomfort each time **THE LITTLE
MONSTER** rears his ugly head.

Get rid of this **MONSTER** – the belief that alcohol does
something for you – and you will be **FREE**.

More importantly, **YOU WON'T FEEL DEPRIVED!!**

Having to **CONSTANTLY FEED THE LITTLE MONSTER**
means that you feel:

MORE STRESSED, MORE OFTEN...

...and your **WELLBEING**
eventually **PLUMMETS
LOWER AND LOWER.**

Yet no matter how low it descends, you **IMAGINE** you feel better each time you feed it.

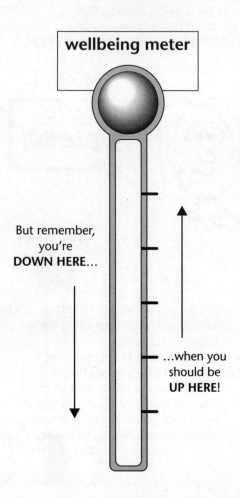

wellbeing meter

But remember, you're **DOWN HERE**...

...when you should be **UP HERE**!

Each drink drags you down **FURTHER** and **FURTHER**.
Over time, the body builds up a tolerance to
ALCOHOL, so when you drink it only **PARTIALLY**
relieves the feeling, so you feel **MORE STRESSED**,
MORE OFTEN and need to **DRINK MORE**.

No matter how
much you feed
the **CRAVING**,
you can never
reach the level of
WELLBEING that
you felt before
you drank.

Even at your best, you will always feel **MORE STRESSED
AND LESS RELAXED** than a non-drinker.

In fact, progressively declining
HEALTH, feelings of **SHAME**,
DISGUST and the **CONSTANT
FEAR** of disease or death looming
in the background ensure that your
feeling of wellbeing keeps sinking
LOWER and **LOWER**.

You do not control the **DRUG**. The drug controls **YOU**.

OK, clearly we need to **EXPLODE** some more **MYTHS**.

Drugs tend to share these common factors:

• We're brainwashed into feeling somehow inadequate and believe the **DRUG** will fill that void in some way.

• The initial dose provides no pleasure or crutch.

• Once the initial dose has worn off, you are fooled into thinking that you cannot become **ADDICTED** – generally the first dose is unpleasant.

• When the drug leaves your system you feel an **INSECURITY** but don't link it to the drug.

• You experience some **RELIEF** from this sensation when you take the drug again.

• This fools you into thinking you are gaining some pleasure from the drug, so you take **MORE**.

ADDICTION:
'Doing something repeatedly that you wish you didn't do at all or did less but cannot'

Here's a test:

HAVE YOU WISHED YOU COULD QUIT OR CUT DOWN BUT COULDN'T?

HAVE YOU ENVIED THOSE WHO CAN ENJOY THEMSELVES WITH LITTLE OR NO ALCOHOL?

DO YOU FEEL YOU HAVE WASTED TIME AND MONEY ON DRINKING?

HAVE YOU FELT DEPRIVED IF YOU HAVEN'T BEEN ABLE TO DRINK AT A LEISURE OR PLEASURE ACTIVITY?

WOULD THE THOUGHT OF NEVER DRINKING AGAIN FILL YOU WITH TERROR?

Oh yes, you're **ADDICTED**.

If you're saying you're drinking out of **HABIT**,
then what you're **REALLY** saying is:

You are not drinking
by **CHOICE**. You are
COMPELLED to drink.
In other words, you are
ADDICTED.

The most pathetic aspect of addiction is:

you continue to take the **DRUG**....

...to be **RID**
of the
FEELING...

...the **DRUG**
created.

The truth is:

**you will NEVER get back to that
feeling of wellbeing
UNTIL you STOP DRINKING.**

You've been experiencing them **ALL
YOUR DRINKING LIFE!!**

And what **CREATED** them?

ALCOHOL

What is there to **MISS**?

The biggest part of the battle is **PSYCHOLOGICAL**.

When you realize that all you're losing is **MISERY**, you're left with only a **TEMPORARY**, mild feeling of insecurity.

Be **HAPPY** because this is an indication that the drug is finally **LEAVING** your system.

So are you ready to
LET IT GO NOW?

Life never gets **LESS**
stressful on drugs – it
only gets **WORSE**.

Alcohol doesn't make a difficult world **BEARABLE** – it makes it a **LIVING HELL**.

Please don't use that as an **EXCUSE** to make the rest of your life the **SAME**.

While getting **PLASTERED** may no longer appeal, you may still think there are **BENEFITS** in moderation.

There AREN'T.

Would you advise a **HEROIN ADDICT** to 'just have one shot every now and then'?

Sorry, but **YES YOU ARE.**

Could you **ABSOLUTELY** guarantee that 'just one drink' wouldn't lead to **ANOTHER**? Tell the **TRUTH**, now!

How quickly would you lose **CONTROL** again?

There's an **EASY WAY** to control alcohol:

DON'T
EVER DRINK
ALCOHOL AGAIN

Nothing **BAD** is happening! How can it be **BAD** for a **NIGHTMARE** to end?

Isn't it **GOOD** to be **FREE**?

What a **RELIEF**!

How can you **MISS** something that did **NOTHING** for you?

It's **OVER**, it's **DONE**.

You have your **LIFE** back.

The Final PREPARATION

By now, you should be **RARING** to **GO!**

Good for **YOU!**

Then somehow you've missed a **VITAL POINT**.

You still think there is some **HIDDEN BENEFIT** to alcohol.

There **ISN'T!**
Read the book again until you '**GET IT**'.

Then you're dithering **UNNECESSARILY!**

What would really be so **HORRIBLE** about never drinking again?

At what point is enough **ENOUGH**?

• When you've **LOST EVERYTHING**?

• When you're **TERMINALLY ILL**?

• When you're **DEAD**?

You have a **PROBLEM** with alcohol.

You don't want to have a **PROBLEM** with alcohol.

You can't have a **PROBLEM** with alcohol if you **DON'T DRINK**!

JUST DO IT! NOW is the time.

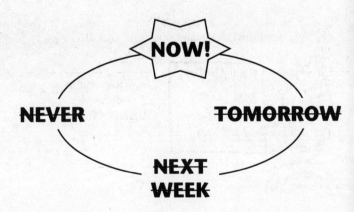

The Final
INSTRUCTIONS

1. Do not think, 'I must not have another drink.' That would create a feeling of deprivation. Instead, start with a feeling of: 'Isn't it great! My life is no longer dominated by **DEVASTATION.**'

2. NEVER, EVER question your decision to stop drinking.

3. Do not try to avoid thinking about alcohol. If you're told not to think of an elephant, guess what's the **FIRST THING** you think about.

4. If over the coming days you ever register an empty insecure feeling of 'I want a drink', don't worry. Instead enjoy the feeling that **YOU** are killing the Little Monster rather than the other way round.

5. Do not mope for a drink. Instead think:

6. Do not **WAIT** to become a non-drinker. You become one the moment you finish that final drink!

7. Accept the fact you will have good and bad days. Remind yourself how much **WORSE** bad days would be if you were still drinking.

8. **YOU** are in control. **YOU** decide what to do with your life.

9. Do not change your **LIFE** just because you've stopped drinking. Do not avoid pubs, restaurants and the company of drinking friends.

10. Enjoy life to the full without alcohol.

THE MOMENT OF REVELATION

Somewhere around this point some people experience what could be called the '**MOMENT OF REVELATION**'.

It is a truly wonderful experience. It is the moment when you know that you are **FREE**.

With some people it happens even before they take the last drink. Perhaps you have already experienced that moment. If not, don't worry. It is important not to try and make that moment happen. Just let it come to you.

It might be after a social occasion or even a trauma; you suddenly realize that not only did you enjoy the occasion or cope with the trauma, but the thought that you no longer drink **NEVER EVEN CROSSED YOUR MIND!**

Your
FINAL
Drink

It may seem strange but we now recommend you have a
FINAL DRINK.

Think of it as a final ritual to mark the **END**
of your drinking life.

More importantly this is a chance to show yourself that it
really **DOES NOTHING** for you any more.

Of course, if you've **ALREADY** abstained for a significant
period, you don't need to have a **DRINK** – just go through
the **RITUAL** of confirming that you've already had your
FINAL DRINK.

However, for current drinkers, this drink marks your **ESCAPE**.

Without it you may sit around wondering whether or not you're really **FREE** yet.

Make it the **STRONGEST, NASTIEST-TASTING** drink you can find.

Now close your eyes
and **TASTE** how **FOUL**
it really is!

Think of all the **MONEY, TIME** and **EMOTION** you
wasted on this disgusting **POISON!**

Make a **SOLEMN VOW**, a **COMMITMENT** to **YOURSELF**
that it will be your **LAST-EVER** alcoholic drink.

Concentrate on the **FOUL TASTE** and ponder how
you were once conned into **PAYING A FORTUNE** to
pour this **FILTHY POISON** down your throat.

At last the whole, horrible **NIGHTMARE** is **OVER!**

137

YOU'VE ACHIEVED WHAT YOU SET OUT TO ACHIEVE: YOU'VE UNLOCKED THAT PRISON DOOR AND CAN NOW ENJOY A HAPPIER, HEALTHIER, MORE FULFILLING LIFE.

YOU'RE FREE FROM THE NIGHTMARE THAT IS THE LIFE OF A DRINKER. REJOICE IN THE FACT THAT YOU ARE FREE.

CONGRATULATIONS!

**NOW GET ON WITH ENJOYING YOUR
AMAZING NEW LIFE!**

TELL ALLEN CARR'S EASYWAY
ORGANISATION THAT YOU'VE ESCAPED
Leave a comment on www.allencarr.com, email
yippee@allencarr.com, like our Facebook page
www.facebook.com/AllenCarr
or write to the Worldwide Head Office address
shown below.

ALLEN CARR'S EASYWAY CLINICS
The following list indicates the countries where
Allen Carr's Easyway To Stop Smoking Clinics
are currently operational. Check www.
allencarr.com for latest additions to this list.
The success rate at the clinics, based on the
three month money-back guarantee, is over 90
per cent.

Selected clinics also offer sessions that deal
with alcohol, other drugs, and weight issues.
Please check with your nearest clinic, listed
below, for details.

Allen Carr's Easyway guarantees that you will
find it easy to stop at the clinics or your money
back.

ALLEN CARR'S EASYWAY
Worldwide Head Office
Park House, 14 Pepys Road, Raynes Park,
London SW20 8NH ENGLAND
Tel: +44 (0)208 9447761
Email: mail@allencarr.com
Website: www.allencarr.com

Worldwide Press Office
Tel: +44 (0)7970 88 44 52
Email: media@allencarr.com

UK Clinic Information and Central Booking
Line 0800 389 2115 (Freephone)

UNITED KINGDOM	JAPAN
REPUBLIC OF IRELAND	LATVIA
AUSTRALIA	LEBANON
AUSTRIA	LITHUANIA
BELGIUM	MAURITIUS
BRAZIL	MEXICO
BULGARIA	NETHERLANDS
CANADA	NEW ZEALAND
CHILE	NORWAY
COLOMBIA	PERU
CYPRUS	POLAND
DENMARK	PORTUGAL
ECUADOR	ROMANIA
ESTONIA	RUSSIA
FINLAND	SERBIA
FRANCE	SINGAPORE
GERMANY	SLOVENIA
GREECE	SOUTH AFRICA
GUATEMALA	SOUTH KOREA
HONG KONG	SPAIN
HUNGARY	SWEDEN
ICELAND	SWITZERLAND
INDIA	TURKEY
ISRAEL	UKRAINE
ITALY	USA

Visit www.allencarr.com to access your
nearest clinic's contact details.

OTHER ALLEN CARR PUBLICATIONS
Allen Carr's revolutionary Easyway method is
available in a wide variety of formats, including
digitally as audiobooks and ebooks, and has been
successfully applied to a broad range of subjects.

For more information about Easyway publications,
please visit
www.easywaypublishing.com

Stop Drinking Now (with hypnotherapy CD)
ISBN: 978-1-84837-982-4

The Easy Way to Control Alcohol
ISBN: 978-1-84837-465-2

No More Hangovers
ISBN: 978-1-84837-555-0

Stop Smoking Now (with hypnotherapy CD)
ISBN: 978-1-84837-373-0

Stop Smoking with Allen Carr (with 70-minute audio CD)
ISBN: 978-1-84858-997-1

The Illustrated Easy Way to Stop Smoking
ISBN: 978-1-84837-930-5

Finally Free!
ISBN: 978-1-84858-979-7

The Easy Way for Women to Stop Smoking
ISBN: 978-1-84837-464-5

The Illustrated Easy Way for Women to Stop Smoking
ISBN: 978-1-78212-495-5

How to Be a Happy Non-Smoker
Ebook

Smoking Sucks (Parent Guide with 16-page comic)
ISBN: 978-0-572-03320-0

No More Ashtrays
ISBN: 978-1-84858-083-1

The Little Book of Quitting
ISBN: 978-1-45490-242-3

The Only Way to Stop Smoking Permanently
ISBN: 978-0-14-024475-1

The Easy Way to Stop Smoking
ISBN: 978-0-71819-455-0

How to Stop Your Child Smoking
ISBN: 978-0-14027-836-1

Lose Weight Now (with hypnotherapy CD)
ISBN: 978-1-84837-720-2

No More Diets
ISBN: 978-1-84837-554-3

The Easyweigh to Lose Weight
ISBN: 978-0-14026-358-9

The Easy Way to Stop Gambling
ISBN: 978-1-78212-448-1

No More Gambling
Ebook

No More Worrying
ISBN: 978-1-84837-826-1

Allen Carr's Get Out of Debt Now
ISBN: 978-1-84837-98-7

No More Debt
Ebook

No More Fear of Flying
ISBN: 978-1-78404-279-0

The Easy Way to Enjoy Flying
ISBN: 978-0-71819-458-3

Burning Ambition
ISBN: 978-0-14103-030-2

The Nicotine Conspiracy
Ebook

Packing It In The Easy Way (the autobiography)
ISBN: 978-0-14101-517-0

DISCOUNT VOUCHER FOR
ALLEN CARR'S EASYWAY CLINICS

Recover the price of this book when
you attend an
Allen Carr's Easyway Clinic
anywhere in the world.

Allen Carr has a global network
of clinics where he guarantees
you will find it easy to stop
smoking or your money back.

The success rate based on this
money-back guarantee is over 90 per cent.

When you book your appointment
mention this voucher and you will
receive a discount to the value
of this book. Contact your
nearest clinic for more information
on how the sessions work and
to book your appointment.
Not valid in conjunction with any other offer.